50 Baking Bliss Recipes

By: Kelly Johnson

Table of Contents

- Chocolate Chip Cookies
- Classic Banana Bread
- Cinnamon Rolls
- Apple Pie
- Lemon Drizzle Cake
- Blueberry Muffins
- Brownies
- Vanilla Cupcakes
- Scones
- Cheesecake
- Pumpkin Bread
- Pecan Pie
- Oatmeal Raisin Cookies
- Red Velvet Cake
- Chocolate Cake
- Almond Croissants
- Raspberry Jam Thumbprint Cookies
- Carrot Cake
- Strawberry Shortcake
- Focaccia Bread
- Churros
- Fruit Galette
- Danish Pastry
- Baked Donuts
- Lemon Meringue Pie
- Baklava
- Chocolate Lava Cake
- Peach Cobbler
- Raspberry Crumble Bars
- Tiramisu
- Chocolate Eclairs
- Puff Pastry Twists
- Bundt Cake
- Brioche Bread
- Chocolate Truffles

- Macarons
- Coconut Macaroons
- Toffee Pudding Cake
- Biscotti
- Madeleines
- Mocha Cake
- Apple Cinnamon Danish
- Poppy Seed Muffins
- Gingerbread Cookies
- Key Lime Pie
- Fruit Tart
- Honey Lavender Cake
- Coconut Cream Pie
- Baked Alaska
- Sweet Potato Pie

Chocolate Chip Cookies

Ingredients:

- 1 cup unsalted butter, softened
- 1 cup granulated sugar
- 1 cup packed brown sugar
- 2 large eggs
- 2 teaspoons vanilla extract
- 3 cups all-purpose flour
- 1 teaspoon baking soda
- 1/2 teaspoon salt
- 2 cups chocolate chips

Instructions:

1. Preheat oven to 350°F (175°C).
2. In a large bowl, cream together butter, granulated sugar, and brown sugar until smooth.
3. Beat in eggs, one at a time, followed by vanilla extract.
4. In a separate bowl, whisk together flour, baking soda, and salt. Gradually add to the wet ingredients.
5. Fold in the chocolate chips.
6. Drop rounded tablespoons of dough onto ungreased baking sheets.
7. Bake for 10-12 minutes or until golden brown. Let cool on sheets for a few minutes before transferring to wire racks to cool completely.

Classic Banana Bread

Ingredients:

- 2 to 3 ripe bananas, mashed
- 1/3 cup melted butter
- 1 teaspoon baking soda
- Pinch of salt
- 3/4 cup granulated sugar
- 1 large egg, beaten
- 1 teaspoon vanilla extract
- 1 1/2 cups all-purpose flour

Instructions:

1. Preheat oven to 350°F (175°C). Grease a loaf pan.
2. In a mixing bowl, mash the bananas with a fork until smooth. Stir in melted butter.
3. Mix in the baking soda and salt. Stir in sugar, beaten egg, and vanilla extract.
4. Add the flour and mix until just combined.
5. Pour the batter into the prepared loaf pan and bake for 60-65 minutes, or until a toothpick comes out clean.
6. Cool in the pan for 10 minutes, then transfer to a wire rack to cool completely.

Cinnamon Rolls

Ingredients:

- 1/2 cup warm milk
- 1/4 cup granulated sugar
- 1 packet active dry yeast
- 1/4 cup unsalted butter, melted
- 2 large eggs
- 4 cups all-purpose flour
- 1 teaspoon salt
- 1/2 cup packed brown sugar
- 2 tablespoons ground cinnamon
- 1/4 cup unsalted butter, softened

Instructions:

1. In a small bowl, combine warm milk, sugar, and yeast. Let sit for 5 minutes until bubbly.
2. In a large bowl, combine flour, salt, and melted butter. Add the eggs and yeast mixture. Mix to form a dough.
3. Knead dough on a floured surface for about 5-7 minutes until smooth.
4. Place dough in a greased bowl, cover with a damp cloth, and let rise for 1 hour.
5. Preheat oven to 375°F (190°C). Roll dough into a rectangle and spread softened butter over the surface.
6. Sprinkle brown sugar and cinnamon over the butter, then roll up the dough and slice into 12 rolls.
7. Place the rolls in a greased baking dish, cover, and let rise for 30 minutes.
8. Bake for 20-25 minutes, or until golden brown. Serve warm.

Apple Pie

Ingredients:

- 6 cups peeled and sliced apples (such as Granny Smith or Honeycrisp)
- 1 tablespoon lemon juice
- 3/4 cup granulated sugar
- 1/4 cup brown sugar
- 1/4 cup all-purpose flour
- 1 teaspoon ground cinnamon
- 1/4 teaspoon ground nutmeg
- 1 tablespoon unsalted butter, cut into small pieces
- 1 package refrigerated pie crusts (or homemade)

Instructions:

1. Preheat oven to 425°F (220°C).
2. In a large bowl, combine sliced apples with lemon juice, sugar, brown sugar, flour, cinnamon, and nutmeg. Toss to coat evenly.
3. Roll out one pie crust and place it in a 9-inch pie dish. Fill with the apple mixture and dot with butter.
4. Cover with the second pie crust, trim the edges, and crimp the edges to seal. Cut slits in the top to allow steam to escape.
5. Bake for 45-50 minutes, until golden brown and the filling is bubbling. Cool before serving.

Lemon Drizzle Cake

Ingredients:

- 1 1/2 cups all-purpose flour
- 1 teaspoon baking powder
- 1/4 teaspoon salt
- 1/2 cup unsalted butter, softened
- 1 cup granulated sugar
- 2 large eggs
- Zest of 1 lemon
- 1/4 cup lemon juice
- 1/4 cup milk

For the drizzle:

- 1/4 cup lemon juice
- 1/2 cup powdered sugar

Instructions:

1. Preheat oven to 350°F (175°C) and grease a loaf pan.
2. In a medium bowl, mix together flour, baking powder, and salt.
3. In a large bowl, cream butter and sugar until light and fluffy. Add eggs one at a time, beating well after each addition.
4. Mix in lemon zest and juice, then gradually add the dry ingredients, alternating with milk.
5. Pour batter into prepared pan and bake for 45-50 minutes, or until a toothpick comes out clean.
6. While the cake is cooling, whisk together lemon juice and powdered sugar to make the drizzle.
7. Once the cake has cooled slightly, drizzle the glaze over the top and let set before serving.

Blueberry Muffins

Ingredients:

- 2 cups all-purpose flour
- 1/2 cup sugar
- 2 teaspoons baking powder
- 1/2 teaspoon salt
- 1/2 cup milk
- 1/4 cup unsalted butter, melted
- 1 large egg
- 1 teaspoon vanilla extract
- 1 1/2 cups fresh blueberries (or frozen)

Instructions:

1. Preheat oven to 375°F (190°C) and line a muffin tin with paper liners.
2. In a large bowl, combine flour, sugar, baking powder, and salt.
3. In a separate bowl, whisk together milk, melted butter, egg, and vanilla extract.
4. Gradually add wet ingredients to dry ingredients and mix until just combined.
5. Gently fold in blueberries.
6. Spoon batter into muffin cups, filling each about 2/3 full.
7. Bake for 18-20 minutes, or until a toothpick comes out clean. Let cool before serving.

Brownies

Ingredients:

- 1/2 cup unsalted butter, melted
- 1 cup granulated sugar
- 2 large eggs
- 1 teaspoon vanilla extract
- 1/3 cup unsweetened cocoa powder
- 1/2 cup all-purpose flour
- 1/4 teaspoon salt
- 1/4 teaspoon baking powder

Instructions:

1. Preheat oven to 350°F (175°C) and grease a 9x9-inch baking pan.
2. In a large bowl, combine melted butter and sugar. Add eggs and vanilla extract, and mix until smooth.
3. Stir in cocoa powder, flour, salt, and baking powder.
4. Pour batter into prepared pan and spread evenly.
5. Bake for 20-25 minutes, or until a toothpick comes out with a few moist crumbs. Let cool before cutting into squares.

Vanilla Cupcakes

Ingredients:

- 1 1/2 cups all-purpose flour
- 1 cup granulated sugar
- 1/2 teaspoon baking powder
- 1/4 teaspoon salt
- 1/2 cup unsalted butter, softened
- 2 large eggs
- 2 teaspoons vanilla extract
- 1/2 cup milk

For frosting:

- 1/2 cup unsalted butter, softened
- 2 cups powdered sugar
- 1 teaspoon vanilla extract
- 1-2 tablespoons milk

Instructions:

1. Preheat oven to 350°F (175°C) and line a muffin tin with paper liners.
2. In a large bowl, mix flour, sugar, baking powder, and salt.
3. In a separate bowl, cream butter, eggs, and vanilla extract. Gradually add the dry ingredients, alternating with milk.
4. Fill cupcake liners 2/3 full with batter.
5. Bake for 15-18 minutes, or until a toothpick comes out clean. Cool completely.
6. For frosting, beat together butter, powdered sugar, vanilla extract, and milk until smooth.
7. Frost cupcakes once they are completely cool.

Scones

Ingredients:

- 2 cups all-purpose flour
- 1/4 cup granulated sugar
- 1 tablespoon baking powder
- 1/2 teaspoon salt
- 1/2 cup unsalted butter, cold and cubed
- 1/2 cup heavy cream
- 1 large egg
- 1 teaspoon vanilla extract
- 1/2 cup currants or raisins (optional)

Instructions:

1. Preheat oven to 400°F (200°C) and line a baking sheet with parchment paper.
2. In a large bowl, combine flour, sugar, baking powder, and salt.
3. Cut in the cold butter until the mixture resembles coarse crumbs.
4. In a separate bowl, whisk together cream, egg, and vanilla extract. Gradually stir into the dry mixture.
5. Fold in currants or raisins if using.
6. Turn dough onto a floured surface and pat into a 1-inch thick circle. Cut into wedges and place on the prepared baking sheet.
7. Bake for 12-15 minutes, or until golden brown.

Cheesecake

Ingredients:

- 1 1/2 cups graham cracker crumbs
- 1/4 cup granulated sugar
- 1/2 cup unsalted butter, melted
- 4 (8 oz) packages cream cheese, softened
- 1 cup granulated sugar
- 3 large eggs
- 1 teaspoon vanilla extract
- 1/4 cup sour cream

Instructions:

1. Preheat oven to 325°F (165°C). Grease a 9-inch springform pan.
2. In a bowl, combine graham cracker crumbs, sugar, and melted butter. Press into the bottom of the pan.
3. Beat cream cheese and sugar together until smooth. Add eggs, one at a time, mixing well after each addition. Stir in vanilla extract and sour cream.
4. Pour the cream cheese mixture over the crust.
5. Bake for 50-60 minutes, or until the center is set.
6. Let cool in the pan for 1 hour before refrigerating for at least 4 hours before serving.

Pumpkin Bread

Ingredients:

- 1 3/4 cups all-purpose flour
- 1 teaspoon baking soda
- 1/2 teaspoon salt
- 1/2 teaspoon ground cinnamon
- 1/4 teaspoon ground nutmeg
- 1/4 teaspoon ground cloves
- 1/2 cup unsalted butter, softened
- 1 cup granulated sugar
- 2 large eggs
- 1 cup canned pumpkin puree
- 1/4 cup water
- 1 teaspoon vanilla extract

Instructions:

1. Preheat oven to 350°F (175°C) and grease a 9x5-inch loaf pan.
2. In a medium bowl, whisk together flour, baking soda, salt, and spices.
3. In a large bowl, cream together butter and sugar until smooth. Add eggs, one at a time, and beat well after each addition.
4. Mix in pumpkin puree, water, and vanilla extract.
5. Gradually add dry ingredients to the wet mixture, mixing until just combined.
6. Pour the batter into the prepared pan and bake for 60-70 minutes, or until a toothpick comes out clean.
7. Cool in the pan for 10 minutes before transferring to a wire rack to cool completely.

Pecan Pie

Ingredients:

- 1 pre-made pie crust (or homemade)
- 1 cup light corn syrup
- 1 cup granulated sugar
- 1/4 teaspoon salt
- 3 large eggs
- 2 tablespoons unsalted butter, melted
- 1 teaspoon vanilla extract
- 1 1/2 cups pecan halves

Instructions:

1. Preheat oven to 350°F (175°C).
2. In a large bowl, whisk together corn syrup, sugar, salt, eggs, butter, and vanilla extract until smooth.
3. Stir in the pecans and mix well.
4. Pour the mixture into the prepared pie crust and spread pecans evenly.
5. Bake for 50-60 minutes, or until the filling is set and golden brown. The center may still be slightly jiggly but will firm up as it cools.
6. Let the pie cool completely before slicing and serving.

Oatmeal Raisin Cookies

Ingredients:

- 1 cup unsalted butter, softened
- 1 cup brown sugar, packed
- 1/2 cup granulated sugar
- 2 large eggs
- 1 teaspoon vanilla extract
- 1 1/2 cups all-purpose flour
- 1 teaspoon baking soda
- 1/2 teaspoon ground cinnamon
- 1/4 teaspoon salt
- 3 cups old-fashioned oats
- 1 1/2 cups raisins

Instructions:

1. Preheat oven to 350°F (175°C) and line baking sheets with parchment paper.
2. In a large bowl, cream together butter, brown sugar, and granulated sugar until smooth.
3. Beat in eggs and vanilla extract.
4. In a separate bowl, whisk together flour, baking soda, cinnamon, and salt.
5. Gradually add the dry ingredients to the wet ingredients and mix until combined.
6. Stir in oats and raisins.
7. Drop rounded tablespoons of dough onto baking sheets and bake for 10-12 minutes, or until golden brown.
8. Cool on the baking sheets for a few minutes before transferring to wire racks to cool completely.

Red Velvet Cake

Ingredients:

- 2 1/2 cups all-purpose flour
- 1 1/2 cups granulated sugar
- 1 teaspoon baking soda
- 1 teaspoon salt
- 1 tablespoon cocoa powder
- 1 1/2 cups vegetable oil
- 1 cup buttermilk, room temperature
- 2 large eggs
- 2 tablespoons red food coloring
- 1 teaspoon vanilla extract
- 1 teaspoon white vinegar

For the cream cheese frosting:

- 8 oz cream cheese, softened
- 1/2 cup unsalted butter, softened
- 4 cups powdered sugar
- 1 teaspoon vanilla extract

Instructions:

1. Preheat oven to 350°F (175°C) and grease and flour two 9-inch round cake pans.
2. In a large bowl, combine flour, sugar, baking soda, salt, and cocoa powder.
3. In a separate bowl, whisk together oil, buttermilk, eggs, food coloring, vanilla extract, and vinegar.
4. Gradually add the wet ingredients to the dry ingredients and mix until smooth.
5. Divide the batter evenly between the prepared cake pans and bake for 30-35 minutes, or until a toothpick comes out clean.
6. Cool the cakes in the pans for 10 minutes, then transfer to wire racks to cool completely.
7. For the frosting, beat cream cheese and butter together until smooth. Gradually add powdered sugar and vanilla extract, beating until fluffy.
8. Frost the cooled cakes with the cream cheese frosting.

Chocolate Cake

Ingredients:

- 1 3/4 cups all-purpose flour
- 1 1/2 cups granulated sugar
- 3/4 cup unsweetened cocoa powder
- 1 1/2 teaspoons baking powder
- 1 1/2 teaspoons baking soda
- 1 teaspoon salt
- 2 large eggs
- 1 cup whole milk
- 1/2 cup vegetable oil
- 2 teaspoons vanilla extract
- 1 cup boiling water

For the chocolate frosting:

- 1/2 cup unsalted butter, softened
- 2/3 cup unsweetened cocoa powder
- 3 cups powdered sugar
- 1/3 cup whole milk
- 1 teaspoon vanilla extract

Instructions:

1. Preheat oven to 350°F (175°C) and grease and flour two 9-inch round cake pans.
2. In a large bowl, whisk together flour, sugar, cocoa powder, baking powder, baking soda, and salt.
3. Add eggs, milk, oil, and vanilla extract, and mix until smooth.
4. Gradually add boiling water, mixing until the batter is well combined (it will be thin).
5. Pour the batter evenly into the prepared cake pans and bake for 30-35 minutes, or until a toothpick comes out clean.
6. Cool the cakes in the pans for 10 minutes, then transfer to wire racks to cool completely.
7. For the frosting, beat butter and cocoa powder together until smooth. Gradually add powdered sugar, milk, and vanilla extract, and beat until fluffy.
8. Frost the cooled cakes with the chocolate frosting.

Almond Croissants

Ingredients:

- 2 cups all-purpose flour
- 1/2 teaspoon salt
- 1 teaspoon instant yeast
- 3/4 cup warm milk
- 1/4 cup granulated sugar
- 3/4 cup unsalted butter, softened
- 1/2 cup almond paste
- 1/4 cup powdered sugar
- 1/4 teaspoon almond extract
- 1 egg, beaten (for egg wash)
- Sliced almonds (for topping)

Instructions:

1. Preheat oven to 375°F (190°C) and line a baking sheet with parchment paper.
2. In a large bowl, combine flour, salt, yeast, warm milk, and sugar. Mix until a dough forms.
3. Knead the dough for about 5 minutes, then cover and let rise for 1-2 hours until doubled in size.
4. Roll the dough into a large rectangle and spread almond paste over the surface. Roll up the dough into a log and slice into individual croissants.
5. Place the croissants on the prepared baking sheet and brush with beaten egg.
6. Sprinkle sliced almonds on top and bake for 15-20 minutes, or until golden brown.
7. Cool slightly before serving.

Raspberry Jam Thumbprint Cookies

Ingredients:

- 1 1/2 cups all-purpose flour
- 1/2 teaspoon baking powder
- 1/4 teaspoon salt
- 1/2 cup unsalted butter, softened
- 1/4 cup granulated sugar
- 1 teaspoon vanilla extract
- 1 large egg yolk
- 1/4 cup raspberry jam

Instructions:

1. Preheat oven to 350°F (175°C) and line baking sheets with parchment paper.
2. In a medium bowl, whisk together flour, baking powder, and salt.
3. In a large bowl, cream together butter and sugar until smooth. Add vanilla extract and egg yolk, and mix until combined.
4. Gradually add the dry ingredients to the wet mixture and mix until a dough forms.
5. Roll dough into 1-inch balls and place them on the prepared baking sheets. Use your thumb to create an indentation in the center of each cookie.
6. Fill each indentation with raspberry jam.
7. Bake for 10-12 minutes, or until the edges are golden. Cool on the baking sheets for a few minutes before transferring to wire racks.

Carrot Cake

Ingredients:

- 2 cups all-purpose flour
- 1 1/2 teaspoons baking powder
- 1 teaspoon baking soda
- 1 1/2 teaspoons ground cinnamon
- 1/2 teaspoon ground nutmeg
- 1/4 teaspoon salt
- 4 large eggs
- 1 1/2 cups granulated sugar
- 1 cup vegetable oil
- 2 teaspoons vanilla extract
- 3 cups grated carrots
- 1 cup chopped walnuts (optional)

For the cream cheese frosting:

- 8 oz cream cheese, softened
- 1/2 cup unsalted butter, softened
- 4 cups powdered sugar
- 1 teaspoon vanilla extract

Instructions:

1. Preheat oven to 350°F (175°C) and grease and flour two 9-inch round cake pans.
2. In a medium bowl, whisk together flour, baking powder, baking soda, cinnamon, nutmeg, and salt.
3. In a large bowl, beat eggs, sugar, oil, and vanilla extract until smooth.
4. Gradually add the dry ingredients to the wet ingredients and mix until combined.
5. Fold in grated carrots and walnuts (if using).
6. Pour the batter evenly into the prepared cake pans and bake for 30-35 minutes, or until a toothpick comes out clean.
7. Cool the cakes in the pans for 10 minutes, then transfer to wire racks to cool completely.
8. For the frosting, beat cream cheese and butter together until smooth. Gradually add powdered sugar and vanilla extract, and beat until fluffy.
9. Frost the cooled cakes with the cream cheese frosting.

Strawberry Shortcake

Ingredients:

- 1 pint fresh strawberries, hulled and sliced
- 2 tablespoons granulated sugar
- 2 cups all-purpose flour
- 1 tablespoon baking powder
- 1/4 teaspoon salt
- 1/4 cup granulated sugar
- 1/2 cup unsalted butter, cold and cubed
- 2/3 cup heavy cream

For the whipped cream:

- 1 cup heavy cream
- 2 tablespoons powdered sugar
- 1 teaspoon vanilla extract

Instructions:

1. Preheat oven to 400°F (200°C) and line a baking sheet with parchment paper.
2. In a bowl, toss sliced strawberries with 2 tablespoons of sugar and set aside.
3. In a large bowl, combine flour, baking powder, salt, and 1/4 cup sugar. Cut in cold butter until the mixture resembles coarse crumbs.
4. Stir in heavy cream until the dough comes together. Turn the dough out onto a floured surface and pat into a 1-inch thick rectangle. Cut into rounds using a biscuit cutter.
5. Place shortcakes on the baking sheet and bake for 12-15 minutes, or until golden brown.
6. For the whipped cream, beat heavy cream, powdered sugar, and vanilla extract until stiff peaks form.
7. To serve, split the shortcakes in half, layer with strawberries and whipped cream, and top with the other half of the shortcake.

Focaccia Bread

Ingredients:

- 2 1/4 teaspoons active dry yeast
- 1 1/2 cups warm water
- 3 tablespoons olive oil, plus extra for drizzling
- 1 teaspoon salt
- 4 cups all-purpose flour
- 1 teaspoon sugar
- 2 teaspoons fresh rosemary, chopped
- Coarse sea salt (for topping)

Instructions:

1. Preheat oven to 400°F (200°C).
2. In a small bowl, dissolve yeast and sugar in warm water. Let sit for 5-10 minutes until foamy.
3. In a large bowl, combine flour, salt, olive oil, and the yeast mixture. Mix until a dough forms.
4. Knead the dough for 5-7 minutes until smooth and elastic.
5. Place the dough in an oiled bowl, cover with a clean towel, and let rise for 1 hour, or until doubled in size.
6. Punch down the dough and transfer to a greased baking sheet. Press the dough into a rectangular shape and dimple with your fingers.
7. Drizzle with olive oil and sprinkle with rosemary and coarse sea salt.
8. Bake for 20-25 minutes, or until golden brown. Let cool slightly before serving.

Churros

Ingredients:

- 1 cup water
- 2 tablespoons granulated sugar
- 1/2 teaspoon salt
- 2 tablespoons unsalted butter
- 1 teaspoon vanilla extract
- 1 cup all-purpose flour
- 2 large eggs
- Vegetable oil (for frying)
- 1/2 cup granulated sugar (for coating)
- 1 teaspoon ground cinnamon

Instructions:

1. In a medium saucepan, combine water, sugar, salt, and butter. Bring to a boil over medium heat.
2. Remove from heat and stir in vanilla extract. Gradually add flour, stirring until the dough comes together.
3. Let the dough cool for about 5 minutes, then beat in the eggs, one at a time, until smooth.
4. Heat vegetable oil in a deep pan to 375°F (190°C).
5. Spoon the dough into a pastry bag fitted with a large star tip.
6. Pipe 4-5 inch strips of dough into the hot oil and fry until golden brown, about 2-3 minutes. Use tongs to remove the churros and place them on a paper towel to drain.
7. In a small bowl, mix together sugar and cinnamon. Coat the warm churros in the cinnamon-sugar mixture and serve immediately.

Fruit Galette

Ingredients:

- 1 pre-made pie crust (or homemade)
- 2 cups mixed fruit (berries, peaches, apples, etc.)
- 1/4 cup granulated sugar
- 1 tablespoon cornstarch
- 1 teaspoon lemon juice
- 1/4 teaspoon ground cinnamon (optional)
- 1 egg (for egg wash)
- 1 tablespoon coarse sugar (for topping)

Instructions:

1. Preheat oven to 375°F (190°C) and line a baking sheet with parchment paper.
2. In a bowl, mix the fruit, granulated sugar, cornstarch, lemon juice, and cinnamon (if using).
3. Roll out the pie dough into a 10-inch circle on a floured surface. Transfer to the prepared baking sheet.
4. Spoon the fruit mixture into the center of the dough, leaving a 1-2 inch border around the edges.
5. Fold the edges of the dough over the fruit to form a rustic crust. Brush the edges with the beaten egg and sprinkle with coarse sugar.
6. Bake for 35-40 minutes, or until the crust is golden and the fruit is bubbly.
7. Let the galette cool slightly before serving.

Danish Pastry

Ingredients:

- 1 package puff pastry (store-bought or homemade)
- 4 oz cream cheese, softened
- 1/4 cup powdered sugar
- 1/2 teaspoon vanilla extract
- 1/2 cup fruit preserves (apricot, raspberry, or blueberry)
- 1 egg (for egg wash)

Instructions:

1. Preheat oven to 375°F (190°C) and line a baking sheet with parchment paper.
2. In a bowl, mix together cream cheese, powdered sugar, and vanilla extract until smooth.
3. Roll out the puff pastry on a floured surface and cut into squares or rectangles.
4. Place a spoonful of cream cheese mixture in the center of each pastry and top with a teaspoon of fruit preserves.
5. Fold the edges of the pastry over the filling to create a pocket. Brush the tops with the beaten egg.
6. Bake for 15-20 minutes, or until golden and puffed.
7. Cool before serving.

Baked Donuts

Ingredients:

- 1 1/2 cups all-purpose flour
- 1 teaspoon baking powder
- 1/2 teaspoon baking soda
- 1/4 teaspoon salt
- 1/2 teaspoon ground cinnamon
- 1/4 cup granulated sugar
- 1 large egg
- 1/2 cup milk
- 2 tablespoons unsalted butter, melted
- 1 teaspoon vanilla extract
- Vegetable oil spray (for greasing)

For the glaze:

- 1 cup powdered sugar
- 2 tablespoons milk
- 1/2 teaspoon vanilla extract

Instructions:

1. Preheat oven to 350°F (175°C) and grease a donut pan with vegetable oil spray.
2. In a bowl, whisk together flour, baking powder, baking soda, salt, cinnamon, and sugar.
3. In a separate bowl, whisk together egg, milk, melted butter, and vanilla extract.
4. Add the wet ingredients to the dry ingredients and mix until just combined.
5. Spoon the batter into the donut pan, filling each mold about 3/4 full.
6. Bake for 10-12 minutes, or until a toothpick comes out clean. Let cool for a few minutes before transferring to a wire rack.
7. For the glaze, whisk together powdered sugar, milk, and vanilla extract. Dip the top of each donut into the glaze and let it set.

Lemon Meringue Pie

Ingredients:

- 1 pre-made pie crust (or homemade)
- 1 1/2 cups granulated sugar
- 1/4 cup cornstarch
- 1/4 teaspoon salt
- 1 1/2 cups water
- 1/2 cup freshly squeezed lemon juice
- 4 large egg yolks
- 2 tablespoons unsalted butter
- 1 teaspoon lemon zest
- 4 large egg whites
- 1/2 teaspoon cream of tartar
- 1/4 cup granulated sugar (for meringue)

Instructions:

1. Preheat oven to 350°F (175°C).
2. In a saucepan, whisk together sugar, cornstarch, and salt. Gradually stir in water and lemon juice.
3. Cook over medium heat, whisking constantly, until the mixture comes to a boil and thickens.
4. In a separate bowl, whisk egg yolks, then slowly add about 1/2 cup of the hot lemon mixture to temper the eggs. Whisk the egg mixture into the saucepan.
5. Continue cooking for 2-3 minutes, then remove from heat. Stir in butter and lemon zest.
6. Pour the filling into the pre-baked pie crust and set aside to cool slightly.
7. For the meringue, beat egg whites and cream of tartar until soft peaks form. Gradually add sugar and beat until stiff peaks form.
8. Spread the meringue over the lemon filling, ensuring it touches the edges of the crust.
9. Bake for 10-12 minutes, or until the meringue is golden brown. Let cool before serving.

Baklava

Ingredients:

- 1 package phyllo dough (16 sheets)
- 2 cups mixed nuts (pistachios, walnuts, almonds), chopped
- 1 teaspoon ground cinnamon
- 1 cup unsalted butter, melted
- 1 cup granulated sugar
- 1 cup water
- 1/2 cup honey
- 1 teaspoon vanilla extract
- 1/2 teaspoon lemon juice

Instructions:

1. Preheat oven to 350°F (175°C) and grease a 9x13-inch baking dish.
2. In a bowl, mix together the chopped nuts and cinnamon.
3. Layer 8 sheets of phyllo dough in the baking dish, brushing each sheet with melted butter.
4. Sprinkle a thin layer of the nut mixture over the phyllo dough.
5. Continue layering phyllo dough and nuts until all the nuts are used, finishing with 8 more layers of phyllo dough.
6. Using a sharp knife, cut the baklava into diamond or square shapes.
7. Bake for 40-45 minutes, or until golden and crisp.
8. While the baklava bakes, prepare the syrup by combining sugar, water, honey, vanilla extract, and lemon juice in a saucepan. Bring to a boil and simmer for 10 minutes.
9. Pour the hot syrup over the baked baklava as soon as it comes out of the oven. Let it soak and cool for a few hours before serving.

Chocolate Lava Cake

Ingredients:

- 1/2 cup unsalted butter
- 4 oz semi-sweet chocolate, chopped
- 1 cup powdered sugar
- 2 large eggs
- 2 large egg yolks
- 1 teaspoon vanilla extract
- 1/4 teaspoon salt
- 1/2 cup all-purpose flour

Instructions:

1. Preheat oven to 425°F (220°C). Grease 4 ramekins with butter and dust with flour.
2. In a saucepan, melt butter and chocolate over medium heat, stirring until smooth.
3. Whisk in powdered sugar, eggs, egg yolks, vanilla extract, and salt until combined.
4. Stir in flour until just incorporated.
5. Pour the batter evenly into the prepared ramekins and bake for 12-14 minutes, or until the edges are set but the center is soft.
6. Let cool for 1 minute before carefully inverting onto plates. Serve immediately with vanilla ice cream or whipped cream.

Peach Cobbler

Ingredients:

- 4 cups fresh or frozen peaches, sliced
- 1/2 cup granulated sugar
- 1 tablespoon cornstarch
- 1 tablespoon lemon juice
- 1 1/2 cups all-purpose flour
- 1/4 cup granulated sugar
- 1 tablespoon baking powder
- 1/4 teaspoon salt
- 1/2 cup unsalted butter, cold and cubed
- 1/2 cup milk
- 1 teaspoon vanilla extract

Instructions:

1. Preheat oven to 375°F (190°C) and grease a 9x9-inch baking dish.
2. In a bowl, mix peaches, sugar, cornstarch, and lemon juice. Pour into the prepared dish.
3. In another bowl, whisk together flour, sugar, baking powder, and salt. Cut in cold butter until the mixture resembles coarse crumbs.
4. Stir in milk and vanilla extract until a dough forms.
5. Drop spoonfuls of dough over the peaches. Bake for 35-40 minutes, or until the top is golden and the filling is bubbly.

Raspberry Crumble Bars

Ingredients:

- **For the crust and crumble:**
    - 1 1/2 cups all-purpose flour
    - 1/2 cup granulated sugar
    - 1/2 teaspoon baking powder
    - 1/4 teaspoon salt
    - 1/2 cup unsalted butter, cold and cubed
    - 1 egg, beaten
- **For the raspberry filling:**
    - 2 cups fresh or frozen raspberries
    - 1/2 cup granulated sugar
    - 1 tablespoon cornstarch
    - 1 tablespoon lemon juice

Instructions:

1. Preheat oven to 350°F (175°C) and grease a 9x9-inch baking pan or line with parchment paper.
2. **For the crust and crumble:** In a medium bowl, mix together the flour, sugar, baking powder, and salt.
3. Cut in the cold butter until the mixture resembles coarse crumbs. Stir in the beaten egg until combined.
4. Press about two-thirds of the dough mixture into the bottom of the prepared pan to form the crust.
5. **For the raspberry filling:** In a bowl, combine raspberries, sugar, cornstarch, and lemon juice. Stir gently until mixed and the berries are coated.
6. Spoon the raspberry mixture over the crust.
7. Sprinkle the remaining dough mixture over the top of the raspberries to form a crumble.
8. Bake for 40-45 minutes, or until the topping is golden brown.
9. Let cool completely in the pan before cutting into bars and serving.

Tiramisu

Ingredients:

- 1 1/2 cups strong brewed coffee, cooled
- 1/2 cup coffee liqueur (optional)
- 6 large egg yolks
- 1 cup granulated sugar
- 1 1/2 cups mascarpone cheese, softened
- 1 1/2 cups heavy cream
- 2 teaspoons vanilla extract
- 1 package ladyfinger cookies (savoiardi)
- Unsweetened cocoa powder (for dusting)
- Dark chocolate (for garnish, optional)

Instructions:

1. In a shallow dish, combine the coffee and coffee liqueur. Set aside.
2. In a medium bowl, whisk the egg yolks and sugar until pale and thick. In another bowl, whisk the mascarpone cheese until smooth.
3. In a separate bowl, whip the heavy cream with vanilla extract until stiff peaks form.
4. Gently fold the mascarpone into the egg yolk mixture, then fold in the whipped cream until smooth and fully combined.
5. Quickly dip each ladyfinger into the coffee mixture (don't soak them too long). Layer the dipped ladyfingers at the bottom of a 9x9-inch or 9x13-inch baking dish.
6. Spread half of the mascarpone mixture over the ladyfingers. Repeat the layers with the remaining ladyfingers and mascarpone mixture.
7. Refrigerate for at least 4 hours, preferably overnight, to allow the flavors to meld.
8. Before serving, dust the top with unsweetened cocoa powder and garnish with grated dark chocolate if desired.

Chocolate Eclairs

Ingredients:

- **For the choux pastry:**
    - 1 cup water
    - 1/2 cup unsalted butter
    - 1 cup all-purpose flour
    - 1/4 teaspoon salt
    - 4 large eggs
- **For the filling:**
    - 2 cups heavy cream
    - 2 tablespoons powdered sugar
    - 1 teaspoon vanilla extract
- **For the chocolate glaze:**
    - 4 oz semi-sweet chocolate, chopped
    - 1/2 cup heavy cream
    - 1 tablespoon unsalted butter

Instructions:

1. **For the choux pastry:** Preheat oven to 400°F (200°C). Line a baking sheet with parchment paper.
2. In a saucepan, combine water and butter. Heat over medium until the butter is melted and the mixture starts to boil.
3. Add the flour and salt, stirring constantly until the dough pulls away from the sides of the pan and forms a ball. Remove from heat and let cool slightly.
4. Beat in the eggs one at a time, fully incorporating each egg before adding the next, until the dough is smooth and shiny.
5. Spoon the dough into a pastry bag fitted with a large round tip and pipe 3-inch long strips onto the prepared baking sheet.
6. Bake for 20-25 minutes, or until the eclairs are puffed and golden. Let cool on a wire rack.
7. **For the filling:** In a bowl, whip the heavy cream with powdered sugar and vanilla extract until stiff peaks form.
8. Using a small knife, make a slit in the side of each eclair and pipe the whipped cream into each one.
9. **For the chocolate glaze:** In a saucepan, heat the heavy cream until it begins to simmer. Remove from heat and stir in the chopped chocolate and butter until smooth.

10. Dip the top of each filled eclair into the chocolate glaze and let set on a wire rack.
11. Refrigerate until ready to serve.

Puff Pastry Twists

Ingredients:

- 1 sheet puff pastry (store-bought or homemade)
- 1/2 cup grated Parmesan cheese
- 1 teaspoon dried oregano
- 1 egg (for egg wash)
- Salt and pepper to taste

Instructions:

1. Preheat oven to 400°F (200°C) and line a baking sheet with parchment paper.
2. Roll out the puff pastry sheet on a floured surface. Brush the top lightly with the beaten egg.
3. Sprinkle Parmesan cheese, oregano, salt, and pepper evenly over the pastry.
4. Cut the pastry into strips (about 1 inch wide) and twist each strip several times.
5. Place the twists on the prepared baking sheet and bake for 10-12 minutes, or until golden and crispy.
6. Serve warm or at room temperature.

Bundt Cake

Ingredients:

- 2 1/2 cups all-purpose flour
- 1 1/2 cups granulated sugar
- 1 teaspoon baking powder
- 1/2 teaspoon baking soda
- 1/2 teaspoon salt
- 1 teaspoon vanilla extract
- 1 cup unsalted butter, softened
- 4 large eggs
- 1 cup sour cream
- 1/4 cup milk

Instructions:

1. Preheat oven to 350°F (175°C). Grease and flour a Bundt cake pan.
2. In a large bowl, whisk together flour, sugar, baking powder, baking soda, and salt.
3. In another bowl, beat together the butter, eggs, vanilla extract, sour cream, and milk until smooth.
4. Gradually add the dry ingredients to the wet mixture and mix until just combined.
5. Pour the batter into the prepared pan and smooth the top.
6. Bake for 45-50 minutes, or until a toothpick inserted into the center comes out clean.
7. Let the cake cool for 10 minutes before transferring to a wire rack to cool completely.

Brioche Bread

Ingredients:

- 3 1/2 cups all-purpose flour
- 1/4 cup granulated sugar
- 1 teaspoon salt
- 1 packet active dry yeast
- 4 large eggs
- 1 cup unsalted butter, softened
- 1/4 cup whole milk, lukewarm
- 1 tablespoon vanilla extract

Instructions:

1. In a bowl, combine flour, sugar, and salt. In another bowl, dissolve yeast in lukewarm milk and let it sit for 5-10 minutes until frothy.
2. Add the yeast mixture, eggs, butter, and vanilla extract to the flour mixture. Stir until the dough comes together.
3. Knead the dough for about 10 minutes until smooth and elastic. Cover the dough and let it rise for 1-2 hours, or until doubled in size.
4. Preheat the oven to 350°F (175°C) and grease a loaf pan.
5. Punch down the dough and shape it into a loaf. Place it in the prepared pan and let it rise again for 30 minutes.
6. Bake for 30-35 minutes, or until the bread is golden and sounds hollow when tapped.
7. Let cool before slicing.

Chocolate Truffles

Ingredients:

- 8 oz dark or semi-sweet chocolate, chopped
- 1/2 cup heavy cream
- 1/2 teaspoon vanilla extract
- Cocoa powder, chopped nuts, or melted chocolate (for coating)

Instructions:

1. In a saucepan, heat the heavy cream over medium heat until it starts to simmer.
2. Remove from heat and pour over the chopped chocolate in a bowl. Let sit for 2-3 minutes to melt.
3. Stir until the chocolate is fully melted and smooth. Add vanilla extract.
4. Let the mixture cool to room temperature, then refrigerate for 1-2 hours, or until firm.
5. Once chilled, use your hands or a melon baller to roll the mixture into small balls.
6. Roll each truffle in cocoa powder, chopped nuts, or dip them in melted chocolate.
7. Refrigerate the truffles for at least 30 minutes before serving.

Macarons

Ingredients:

- 1 1/2 cups powdered sugar
- 1 cup almond flour
- 3 large egg whites, at room temperature
- 1/4 cup granulated sugar
- 1/2 teaspoon vanilla extract
- Buttercream or ganache (for filling)

Instructions:

1. Preheat oven to 300°F (150°C) and line two baking sheets with parchment paper.
2. In a food processor, sift together the powdered sugar and almond flour until fine.
3. In a mixing bowl, beat egg whites until soft peaks form. Gradually add granulated sugar and continue beating until stiff peaks form.
4. Gently fold the dry ingredients into the egg whites, being careful not to deflate the mixture.
5. Transfer the batter to a piping bag and pipe small circles onto the prepared baking sheets.
6. Let the piped macarons rest for 30 minutes, or until they form a skin.
7. Bake for 15-20 minutes, or until the shells are firm and easy to peel off.
8. Cool the macarons completely before filling with buttercream or ganache.

Coconut Macaroons

Ingredients:

- 2 cups sweetened shredded coconut
- 2 large egg whites
- 1/4 cup granulated sugar
- 1/2 teaspoon vanilla extract
- A pinch of salt

Instructions:

1. Preheat oven to 325°F (160°C) and line a baking sheet with parchment paper.
2. In a mixing bowl, combine coconut, egg whites, sugar, vanilla extract, and salt.
3. Stir until the mixture is well combined and sticky.
4. Using your hands or a spoon, form small mounds of coconut mixture and place them on the baking sheet.
5. Bake for 15-18 minutes, or until the macaroons are golden brown on the edges.
6. Let cool before serving.

Toffee Pudding Cake

Ingredients:

- 1 cup all-purpose flour
- 1/2 cup granulated sugar
- 1 teaspoon baking powder
- 1/2 teaspoon salt
- 1/2 cup whole milk
- 1/4 cup unsalted butter, melted
- 1 large egg
- 1 teaspoon vanilla extract
- 1 cup brown sugar
- 1 cup boiling water

Instructions:

1. Preheat oven to 350°F (175°C) and grease a 9-inch baking dish.
2. In a bowl, whisk together flour, sugar, baking powder, and salt.
3. Add milk, butter, egg, and vanilla extract and mix until smooth.
4. Pour the batter into the prepared dish.
5. In a separate bowl, combine brown sugar and boiling water. Pour this mixture over the batter (do not stir).
6. Bake for 30-35 minutes, or until the cake has risen and is golden brown.
7. Serve warm with whipped cream or vanilla ice cream.

Biscotti

Ingredients:

- 2 cups all-purpose flour
- 1 cup granulated sugar
- 1 teaspoon baking powder
- 1/4 teaspoon salt
- 2 large eggs
- 1 teaspoon vanilla extract
- 1/2 cup almonds, chopped (optional)

Instructions:

1. Preheat oven to 350°F (175°C) and line a baking sheet with parchment paper.
2. In a bowl, combine flour, sugar, baking powder, and salt.
3. In another bowl, beat eggs and vanilla extract.
4. Gradually add the wet ingredients to the dry ingredients and mix until combined. Fold in almonds if desired.
5. Divide the dough in half and shape each half into a log about 2 inches wide.
6. Bake for 25-30 minutes, or until golden. Let cool for 10 minutes.
7. Slice each log into 1-inch pieces and return to the baking sheet.
8. Bake for an additional 10-12 minutes to crisp up the biscotti.

Madeleines

Ingredients:

- 1/2 cup unsalted butter, melted
- 3/4 cup all-purpose flour
- 1 teaspoon baking powder
- 1/2 teaspoon salt
- 2 large eggs
- 1/2 cup granulated sugar
- 1 teaspoon vanilla extract
- Zest of 1 lemon (optional)

Instructions:

1. Preheat oven to 375°F (190°C) and grease a madeleine pan.
2. In a bowl, sift together flour, baking powder, and salt.
3. In another bowl, whisk together eggs and sugar until pale and fluffy.
4. Gently fold in the dry ingredients, melted butter, vanilla extract, and lemon zest.
5. Spoon the batter into the madeleine pan, filling each mold about 3/4 full.
6. Bake for 10-12 minutes, or until the edges are golden and the center springs back when touched.
7. Let the madeleines cool slightly before removing from the pan.

Mocha Cake

Ingredients:

- 1 1/2 cups all-purpose flour
- 1 cup granulated sugar
- 1/2 cup unsweetened cocoa powder
- 1 teaspoon baking powder
- 1/2 teaspoon baking soda
- 1/2 teaspoon salt
- 1 cup brewed coffee (cooled)
- 1/2 cup vegetable oil
- 2 large eggs
- 1 teaspoon vanilla extract

Instructions:

1. Preheat oven to 350°F (175°C) and grease and flour a cake pan.
2. In a bowl, whisk together flour, sugar, cocoa powder, baking powder, baking soda, and salt.
3. In a separate bowl, mix together coffee, vegetable oil, eggs, and vanilla extract.
4. Add the wet ingredients to the dry ingredients and mix until smooth.
5. Pour the batter into the prepared pan and bake for 30-35 minutes, or until a toothpick comes out clean.
6. Let the cake cool completely before frosting or serving.

Churros

Ingredients:

- 1 cup water
- 2 tablespoons granulated sugar
- 1/2 teaspoon salt
- 2 tablespoons unsalted butter
- 1 teaspoon vanilla extract
- 1 cup all-purpose flour
- 2 large eggs
- Vegetable oil (for frying)
- 1/2 cup granulated sugar (for coating)
- 1 teaspoon ground cinnamon

Instructions:

1. In a medium saucepan, combine water, sugar, salt, and butter. Bring to a boil over medium heat.
2. Remove from heat and stir in vanilla extract. Gradually add flour, stirring until the dough comes together.
3. Let the dough cool for about 5 minutes, then beat in the eggs, one at a time, until smooth.
4. Heat vegetable oil in a deep pan to 375°F (190°C).
5. Spoon the dough into a pastry bag fitted with a large star tip.
6. Pipe 4-5 inch strips of dough into the hot oil and fry until golden brown, about 2-3 minutes. Use tongs to remove the churros and place them on a paper towel to drain.
7. In a small bowl, mix together sugar and cinnamon. Coat the warm churros in the cinnamon-sugar mixture and serve immediately.

Fruit Galette

Ingredients:

- 1 pre-made pie crust (or homemade)
- 2 cups mixed fruit (berries, peaches, apples, etc.)
- 1/4 cup granulated sugar
- 1 tablespoon cornstarch
- 1 teaspoon lemon juice
- 1/4 teaspoon ground cinnamon (optional)
- 1 egg (for egg wash)
- 1 tablespoon coarse sugar (for topping)

Instructions:

1. Preheat oven to 375°F (190°C) and line a baking sheet with parchment paper.
2. In a bowl, mix the fruit, granulated sugar, cornstarch, lemon juice, and cinnamon (if using).
3. Roll out the pie dough into a 10-inch circle on a floured surface. Transfer to the prepared baking sheet.
4. Spoon the fruit mixture into the center of the dough, leaving a 1-2 inch border around the edges.
5. Fold the edges of the dough over the fruit to form a rustic crust. Brush the edges with the beaten egg and sprinkle with coarse sugar.
6. Bake for 35-40 minutes, or until the crust is golden and the fruit is bubbly.
7. Let the galette cool slightly before serving.

Danish Pastry

Ingredients:

- 1 package puff pastry (store-bought or homemade)
- 4 oz cream cheese, softened
- 1/4 cup powdered sugar
- 1/2 teaspoon vanilla extract
- 1/2 cup fruit preserves (apricot, raspberry, or blueberry)
- 1 egg (for egg wash)

Instructions:

1. Preheat oven to 375°F (190°C) and line a baking sheet with parchment paper.
2. In a bowl, mix together cream cheese, powdered sugar, and vanilla extract until smooth.
3. Roll out the puff pastry on a floured surface and cut into squares or rectangles.
4. Place a spoonful of cream cheese mixture in the center of each pastry and top with a teaspoon of fruit preserves.
5. Fold the edges of the pastry over the filling to create a pocket. Brush the tops with the beaten egg.
6. Bake for 15-20 minutes, or until golden and puffed.
7. Cool before serving.

Baked Donuts

Ingredients:

- 1 1/2 cups all-purpose flour
- 1 teaspoon baking powder
- 1/2 teaspoon baking soda
- 1/4 teaspoon salt
- 1/2 teaspoon ground cinnamon
- 1/4 cup granulated sugar
- 1 large egg
- 1/2 cup milk
- 2 tablespoons unsalted butter, melted
- 1 teaspoon vanilla extract
- Vegetable oil spray (for greasing)

For the glaze:

- 1 cup powdered sugar
- 2 tablespoons milk
- 1/2 teaspoon vanilla extract

Instructions:

1. Preheat oven to 350°F (175°C) and grease a donut pan with vegetable oil spray.
2. In a bowl, whisk together flour, baking powder, baking soda, salt, cinnamon, and sugar.
3. In a separate bowl, whisk together egg, milk, melted butter, and vanilla extract.
4. Add the wet ingredients to the dry ingredients and mix until just combined.
5. Spoon the batter into the donut pan, filling each mold about 3/4 full.
6. Bake for 10-12 minutes, or until a toothpick comes out clean. Let cool for a few minutes before transferring to a wire rack.
7. For the glaze, whisk together powdered sugar, milk, and vanilla extract. Dip the top of each donut into the glaze and let it set.

Lemon Meringue Pie

Ingredients:

- 1 pre-made pie crust (or homemade)
- 1 1/2 cups granulated sugar
- 1/4 cup cornstarch
- 1/4 teaspoon salt
- 1 1/2 cups water
- 1/2 cup freshly squeezed lemon juice
- 4 large egg yolks
- 2 tablespoons unsalted butter
- 1 teaspoon lemon zest
- 4 large egg whites
- 1/2 teaspoon cream of tartar
- 1/4 cup granulated sugar (for meringue)

Instructions:

1. Preheat oven to 350°F (175°C).
2. In a saucepan, whisk together sugar, cornstarch, and salt. Gradually stir in water and lemon juice.
3. Cook over medium heat, whisking constantly, until the mixture comes to a boil and thickens.
4. In a separate bowl, whisk egg yolks, then slowly add about 1/2 cup of the hot lemon mixture to temper the eggs. Whisk the egg mixture into the saucepan.
5. Continue cooking for 2-3 minutes, then remove from heat. Stir in butter and lemon zest.
6. Pour the filling into the pre-baked pie crust and set aside to cool slightly.
7. For the meringue, beat egg whites and cream of tartar until soft peaks form. Gradually add sugar and beat until stiff peaks form.
8. Spread the meringue over the lemon filling, ensuring it touches the edges of the crust.
9. Bake for 10-12 minutes, or until the meringue is golden brown. Let cool before serving.

Baklava

Ingredients:

- 1 package phyllo dough (16 sheets)
- 2 cups mixed nuts (pistachios, walnuts, almonds), chopped
- 1 teaspoon ground cinnamon
- 1 cup unsalted butter, melted
- 1 cup granulated sugar
- 1 cup water
- 1/2 cup honey
- 1 teaspoon vanilla extract
- 1/2 teaspoon lemon juice

Instructions:

1. Preheat oven to 350°F (175°C) and grease a 9x13-inch baking dish.
2. In a bowl, mix together the chopped nuts and cinnamon.
3. Layer 8 sheets of phyllo dough in the baking dish, brushing each sheet with melted butter.
4. Sprinkle a thin layer of the nut mixture over the phyllo dough.
5. Continue layering phyllo dough and nuts until all the nuts are used, finishing with 8 more layers of phyllo dough.
6. Using a sharp knife, cut the baklava into diamond or square shapes.
7. Bake for 40-45 minutes, or until golden and crisp.
8. While the baklava bakes, prepare the syrup by combining sugar, water, honey, vanilla extract, and lemon juice in a saucepan. Bring to a boil and simmer for 10 minutes.
9. Pour the hot syrup over the baked baklava as soon as it comes out of the oven. Let it soak and cool for a few hours before serving.

Chocolate Lava Cake

Ingredients:

- 1/2 cup unsalted butter
- 4 oz semi-sweet chocolate, chopped
- 1 cup powdered sugar
- 2 large eggs
- 2 large egg yolks
- 1 teaspoon vanilla extract
- 1/4 teaspoon salt
- 1/2 cup all-purpose flour

Instructions:

1. Preheat oven to 425°F (220°C). Grease 4 ramekins with butter and dust with flour.
2. In a saucepan, melt butter and chocolate over medium heat, stirring until smooth.
3. Whisk in powdered sugar, eggs, egg yolks, vanilla extract, and salt until combined.
4. Stir in flour until just incorporated.
5. Pour the batter evenly into the prepared ramekins and bake for 12-14 minutes, or until the edges are set but the center is soft.
6. Let cool for 1 minute before carefully inverting onto plates. Serve immediately with vanilla ice cream or whipped cream.

Peach Cobbler

Ingredients:

- 4 cups fresh or frozen peaches, sliced
- 1/2 cup granulated sugar
- 1 tablespoon cornstarch
- 1 tablespoon lemon juice
- 1 1/2 cups all-purpose flour
- 1/4 cup granulated sugar
- 1 tablespoon baking powder
- 1/4 teaspoon salt
- 1/2 cup unsalted butter, cold and cubed
- 1/2 cup milk
- 1 teaspoon vanilla extract

Instructions:

1. Preheat oven to 375°F (190°C) and grease a 9x9-inch baking dish.
2. In a bowl, mix peaches, sugar, cornstarch, and lemon juice. Pour into the prepared dish.
3. In another bowl, whisk together flour, sugar, baking powder, and salt. Cut in cold butter until the mixture resembles coarse crumbs.
4. Stir in milk and vanilla extract until a dough forms.
5. Drop spoonfuls of dough over the peaches. Bake for 35-40 minutes, or until the top is golden and the filling is bubbly.

www.ingramcontent.com/pod-product-compliance
Lightning Source LLC
LaVergne TN
LVHW061953070526
838199LV00060B/4092